LEGAL

NOTE: Some of the recipes in this book include raw eggs. Raw eggs may contain bacteria. It is recommended that you purchase certified salmonella-free eggs from a reliable source and store them in the refrigerator. You should not feed raw eggs to babies or small kids. Likewise, pregnant women, elderly persons, or those with a compromised immune system should not eat raw eggs. Neither the author nor the publisher claims responsibility for adverse effects resulting from the use of the recipes and/or information found within this book.

By: A.J. Luigi

INTRODUCTION

We've Got THE BEST CRISPY CRUSTS PIZZA'S in the Pizza Game!

Everyone loves pizza and what better way to get any meal going than to do these three simple steps that we've made for you in this booklet. Just read the steps and see how easy making these pizza's can be!
Make sure to read our care section for your pizza stone so that you get the most out of your product!

Our Simple 1, 2, 3 Method Below is for Making the Best Pizza You've Ever Had!

Step 1: Choose Your Favorite Crust.
Step 2: Pick Your Best Sauce.
Step 3: Choose from a List Toppings!

Pizza should be fun and done the right way. That's why we've put these recipes together for you to choose the type of crust you want. Then we have a variety of sauces that we thought you'd love to choose from. Then the toppings are endless! These simple and easy to make recipes will have you cooking like you're a "TOP CHEF" right in the comfort of your own home. Enjoy pizza stone cooking just like it came from the ovens of an Italian Chef! It's fun and easy, so impress your friends, family and loved ones, and do it in a healthy way!

TABLE OF CONTENTS

Pizza Stone Recipe Cookbook

SECTION 1:
IT'S ALL ABOUT THE STONE!

A PIZZA STONE'S PURPOSE

What is the dream of all amateur chefs? Making pizza at home! Well maybe it's not *everyone's* dream, but it certainly adds an amazing dynamic to your culinary repertoire! Imagine having an Italian bistro right in your home, serving one of the most beloved dishes worldwide – without all the tourists and the fact you have to pay for dinner of course.

We will delve into pizza ingredients – which you will find are incredibly basic and common – a little later on, but we need to start with the right equipment. The most essential piece for creating restaurant-style pizza at home is a pizza stone!

A pizza stone – or *baking stone* as it's referred to – has its many benefits. Your pizza is evenly cooked throughout, it gives the pie a crispier crust than if cooked on just an ordinary baking sheet, and it mimics the result of a main course that comes directly from a brick oven at your favorite pizza joint.

Of course, it would be ideal if you could have a fancy masonry oven in your kitchen. However, we both know you're not that crafty and not that rich. And if you were, you might as well just have a personal chef and there would be no reason to read this book. For everyone else, it's time to get your hands in the dough and enjoy your classic creation!

THE STYLE ISN'T SET IN STONE

You wouldn't think there would be multiple choices for a pizza stone. I mean, all it is, is a stone slab you stick in your oven. However, it's a product and we live in a world of capitalism and competition. Just like there are many different places to go out and eat pizza, there are many different options to make pizza at home.

The easy choice is the shape. There are really only three you want to choose from: square, rectangle, or circle. Now, we also live in a world of creativity and expression so maybe someone out there designed a triangle or trapezoid or something, but try to avoid the novelty and stick with something practical.

Second, make sure the shape fits your oven BEFORE you buy it. A 16" x 14" is generally the largest stone you will find on the market (for home use), but what you want to do is measure your oven (hopefully while it's off – I don't want to be forced to say that, but I have to) and make sure you pick a stone that fits 1" from each side for safety and air circulation.

Now the material. Your choices will most likely be clay, cast iron, or steel. They all have their pros and cons. A clay stone offers more variety for sizes and price ranges and keeps the cooking consistent, but it does take the longest to heat and has the slim possibility of cracking. A cast iron stone heats quicker and cooks the pizza perfectly, but is heavy and depending on the style, may have a lip that makes it difficult to slide the pie in and out. The steel stone is high-end and cooks your dish the quickest and the best, but is very heavy and also very expensive.

As you can see, the cons are not necessarily deal breakers, and the pros are worth whatever stone you choose. The last piece of advice is to get a thicker stone for better heat absorption – best would be a thickness of ¾"-1".

You have your stone, and now you just have to use it!

EASY AS PIZZA PIE TO USE

It's very easy to use: just heat up, slide the pizza on, and wait impatiently for less than 20 minutes! Okay there's more to it than that. You're in this for the education, remember? Don't worry, you don't have to go back to school and deal with dreadful textbooks and homework – this is hands-on fun!

Let's start with how the pizza stone actually works. It's designed to drain and absorb the water from the dough. This creates the crispy crust. Also, and perhaps its main purpose, is to heat the pie thoroughly and evenly by providing a consistent, lasting high temperature. The initial burst from the heat puffs up the crust and at the end leaves the perfect amount of char underneath for a home-style delight.

The best part of a pizza stone is the fact it's so simple for anyone to use. It essentially stays in your oven – preferably used on the lower rack. No, really, that's all it does. First, make sure your dough has risen and is at room-temperature (it will be). Depending on the style of stone described in the last section, you will preheat the oven to your desired cooking temperature and let your stone heat up for at least 30 minutes. I know, it sounds like a waste of resources, but so is wasting gas and polluting the environment driving to a restaurant. We're not going to get into the touchy topic of "being green"; we're trying to have fun here. After the oven is nice and toasty, slide your put-together pie onto the stone with a pizza peel.

Let cook. Carefully slide off stone. Enjoy Pizza. See, it's simple!

SECTION 2: EVERYONE LOVES PIZZA

A SOCIETY OBSESSED

Where and when did this pizza craze begin? Well, where most delicious cuisine comes from: Italy – Naples to be exact. It was during the 1700's when the town was growing and street vendors began offering a cheap flatbread with toppings. Legend had it that it sparked the attention of King Umberto I and Queen Margharita as they were passing through, and from then on it became more popular.

Did it ever! The world became enthralled with this basic creation. In 1905, G. Lombardi's opened in Manhattan, becoming the first registered pizza join in America. During World War II, a migration across the country brought a wave of business west. You can probably fill in what happened next.

No? Okay, I will make it easy on you. We became obsessed! From expansion to delivery to hipster trends, pizza has been a cornerstone of dining out. It's easy, it's cheap, and it's quick. You can get it in a pinch or when you're feeling lazy, it can be consumed alone or by the masses at huge gatherings, and it can be made in every way possible.

Now it's even easier to make at home. What else can be done? Remember when "picture in picture" came out on televisions and you were like, "No way, the future is here, there's no way they can top that?" Pizza keeps progressing as well, and stays true to its roots. What I'm trying to say is why isn't "picture in picture" a thing anymore? It was amazing! No, wait, that's not what I'm trying to say. We're obsessed all right.

By: A.J. Luigi

DON'T GIVE PIZZA A BAD NAME; IT DIDN'T DO ANYTHING

It's hard to find someone who doesn't enjoy pizza, and if they don't, they're probably lying and you shouldn't affiliate yourself with liars. The reason I say that is because you can make a pizza every which way, healthy or non-healthy. If they have an excuse, you have an answer.

I heard, and then always like to repeat, that a pizza can contain the four major food groups in every bite. Of course, trends have altered the structure of the food pyramid with new allergies and diseases evolving as well as yet another super food being pushed. I mean, I guess you could make a soy cheese, quinoa, and kale pizza with a gluten-free crust, but that's you're thing, definitely not mine. I'm lactose intolerant and I still have classic mozzarella on my pie. I just keep the good people over at Lactaid in business. My point is that you can benefit from what many automatically claim to be an unhealthy food.

The best way to make sure you're getting everything you want, whether that be your weird toppings or your healthy alternative, is to make the pizza at home. You're given a blank canvas when you make your dough and you can do anything you please. Also, generally speaking, you tend to have less grease when cooking at home because you can control the amount of ingredients you use. You have the ability to control the health level, don't go blaming the pizza! It doesn't know any better.

So be healthy, be unhealthy, be creative, and have fun making the pizza you want at home!

PIZZA HELPERS

There are helpers all around you. Where I live I have 8 pizza joints within a mile radius. I'm not exaggerating. However, it's wonderful to have options and it's convenient when I don't feel like cooking – not to mention some of them are top-notch. Of course, the major chains are also included in that list, but sometimes you just don't want to get off the couch. If I was a more trusting person I would just leave my door unlocked and tell the driver to come in and place the pizza in front of me, maybe even present a slice to my mouth. Okay, we've gone too far. Convenience is one thing; severe laziness is another.

Don't be lazy. Making pizza at home isn't as difficult as it would seem. I'm not talking about the fast take n' bake pizzas or purchasing dough from your local pie restaurant either. I'm talking about making the dough with the basic ingredients of flour, yeast, water, salt, and oil. I'm talking about getting your hands and kitchen dirty and making it worth it.

Forego the outside help and use the tools you have at home. You will need a food processor for your dough. If you don't have one then you can do it the old-fashioned way with your mitts. It won't take long and will be more rewarding if you're into showing off. Then you just need your basic measuring cups and spoons, ingredients, and a small plastic bag. I use an empty produce bag from my trip to the grocery store.

Lastly, get your pizza stone; it makes a world of difference! But if you need some extra hands, you have options.

BACHIN' IT

I lived on my own for a little under a decade before meeting my wife. No roommates or anything. It was great (don't tell my wife that), but despite all my hobbies, there was some downtime to say the least. Cooking was a great release, therapeutic almost.

I learned to make pizza from my mom and it was quite beneficial; it's almost comparable to someone teaching you to learn how to fish – kind of. If I had a little time on a Friday night or Saturday afternoon I could make a pizza and essentially have food for the weekend.

So, if you live alone and have some time on your hands then put some music on (it doesn't necessarily have to be Italian opera), tie an apron around your waist, and get to work. You could have a masterpiece made and be sitting on the couch, eating dinner, drinking a beer, and watching sports or playing video games.

I guess you just got a glimpse of my bachelor life. Not bad, eh?

FREE FAMILY LABOR

Now you have a family and suddenly less time each passing day. The one downfall to making your own pizza from scratch is it does take a little bit of time. You're going to want the dough to rise at least an hour after making it, and it takes a little to complete in the first place if you don't have a food processor. Where the heck is the time if you have a family to tend to as well?

Free labor. You knew you had kids for a reason. I mentioned that my mom taught me how to make pizza, and it was at a young age; it was fun for me because I was involved. I was probably also a tad oblivious to the fact I was being used as well, but I didn't seem to mind, and neither will your kids.

Think about it from a kid's perspective; it's a messy process with flour dusting the counters and cooks, they get your attention and you get to hang out with them (this is obviously before they become annoying teenagers), and they are being creative and love the end product. All good things! Now, if you can convince them that doing the dishes is fun then you might not even have to lift a finger.

Pizza has been a staple of family dinners for a very long time, and it will always remain that way. Instead of ordering out, make it an event and bond in the kitchen.

THAT'S AMORE

Learning to cook as a child is such a wonderful experience because it gives you a useful trait later in life. First, it saves you money; second, you can be a little healthier; third, it promotes creativity and keeps the mind busy; and fourth, it impresses your partner or someone you're in the midst of courting.

Making pizza together is a great date night for a couple. Don't worry, we're going to keep this PG-13 and in the kitchen (not that that matters for some). Whoa! Calm down now. I said it would be PG-13 so some speculation can be assumed. Let's just keep our hands in the dough and get back on track.

Pizza can be made solo, but it's a perfect dish for a team effort as well. One could sauce, the other could sprinkle the cheese. One could spread the toppings, the other could slide it onto the pizza stone. And then the man probably has to clean up. The date is fun, unique, and brings the couple closer and keeps them off their phones – and then with the help of the pizza stone a restaurant-quality dinner is to follow – and then maybe a movie on the couch – and then maybe... Onto the next situation!

PIZZA PARTY

Yes, pizza parties are usually for children, but why do they get all the fun? Let's say you're a grown-up (age doesn't necessarily qualify you as such). You're probably social and have a solid couple of friends you can rely on. It doesn't matter if you live alone or have a family or it's just you and your partner, sometimes you just need a night out (or in) with the guys or gals.

A pizza night will do the trick! Grab your drinks and begin your play lists, start a little early, and get cooking. You get to stay home with your close friends, act dumb because you can, dress in comfy clothes because you don't need to impress anyone, and maybe even start a friendly competition: who can make the best pizza pie – or even the most creative? Most pizza stones can hold at least four small personal pizzas!

Not to sound like a corporate drone, but it's a great team-building exercise. Just like with your family or partner, it will bring the group together. Also, and this goes for any of the above situations, pizza is a very mobile food. You can do anything with a piece of pie in your hand. So, if the pizza is ready and you're having a game or movie night, there's no reason to halt the activity and gather around a dining room table if you don't want to. Just have some fun and go with the flow!

SECTION 3: GET CREATIVE

IMAGINE ALL THE PIZZA

Why do you think that the Teenage Mutant Ninja Turtles were named after Italian artists and loved pizza? I think the answer is pretty obvious: making pizza is a work of art. That was a stretch, but we're going to go with it.

So, you have your dough and it's rolled out, just sitting there, naked and a little confused of why it isn't dressed in deliciousness yet. Nowadays there is no standard to what you can do, but we will start with the basics: sauce and cheese.

For traditionalists such as myself, I like the classic tomato pizza sauce. While cooking with a pizza stone, don't be shy with the amount you use as well. Also, don't be tempted to buy the expensive brands when you can doctor-up a cheaper version.

Here's a freebie: buy a generic sauce, sauté some minced garlic in olive oil, add a little pepper and oregano, and combine. People have used other sauces like pesto (another favorite), BBQ sauce, and even hummus amongst other wild experiments. Cooking at home allows you to choose!

Next is the cheese and the same applies! Cheese is probably the most important topping though. Again, you can go the traditional route and use mozzarella, or you can try something different like cheddar (goes great with a BBQ base) or provolone to really make it extra-Italian. So you have your first two layers. Now what?

IF I WANT ANCHOVIES, I'LL HAVE ANCHOVIES

Anything. Seriously, anything. It's great to use your imagination, but my best advice would be to make sure things go well smothered in cheese or make sure they pair well with each other. You will be surprised that most things work though!

Don't forget that extra cheese is a topping! Yes, that is coming from someone who admitted being lactose intolerant. You can combine cheeses like mozzarella and cheddar, and even give an extra light layer of Parmesan on top before sliding the pizza onto your stone. It's not just for garnishing after the fact.

Another freebie: put a light layer of cheese after the sauce, then some toppings to soak up a little of the flavor from your base, then the rest of the cheese so the toppings are slightly buried – and then, of course, another layer of toppings!

One of my favorite combinations is very simple and it was inspired during one of our annual Halloween parties. We wanted to keep the theme, but nothing people wouldn't eat, so went with Halloween colors using cheddar cheese and black olives. We actually make that pizza quite often now because it was so good.

The list of possibilities is quite long; be creative, be thematic, be inspired. Think of another food and how it is made. If you want a hamburger pizza, use cheddar and ground beef; if you want to add to that BBQ pizza from the last section, use chicken and red onions; if you want to make a delicious pesto pizza, put spinach and artichoke hearts on top. Hopefully you're catching on.

Your pizza stone will cook anything you put on it will come out perfectly. So again, don't be shy!

NO REASON TO SKIP THE CRUST ANYMORE

Just like people have different tastes in sauce, cheese, and toppings, they also prefer different styles of crust. This is where the pizza stone comes in handy once again!

The stone generally makes the crust crispier and a little charred which is how it's done in masonry ovens. However, not everyone is into that, but don't worry, your stone doesn't just cook one way!

A pizza stone will get you something very close to a Neapolitan crust on a consist basis. That means it's going to be thin and crusty, but it doesn't have to be. You control the thickness of your dough when you're rolling it out. So if you want something similar to a St. Louis style, then make the dough extra thin and the stone will make it very crispy.

This brings us to our next technique: time cooked. The longer you cook the dough the crispier it's going to get. Also, the thicker the dough, the longer it will take for your desired crispiness – if that's what you're after. For example, if you want New York style, you want the crust to be slightly crispy to soft, so make it kind of thick, maybe ½", and set the timer for a minute or two less. To mimic a pan crust, try ¾".

Some people like it dense though. For a Sicilian crust, you want to make it around 1" thick and if you want the classic deep-dish style, make it 2" thick. A cast-iron stone may be ideal because they tend to have a lip and can handle the higher crust.

Also, don't forget to give your crust more flavor by brushing some garlic butter and a sprinkle of seasoning before putting it on the stone!

HEALTH NUTS CAN USE HEALTHY NUTS

Many people would like to stay healthy though; some even avoiding eating the crust altogether! We don't want to waste food though, do we?

For the crust, a good alternative to the deep-dish covered in garlic butter (eesh) is flatbread. This style is growing in popularity and it doesn't leave much of a bready border around your toppings. More toppings without the guilt! You can try smaller portions by making French bread pizzas, or even using pita bread for personal sizes. Others would like to avoid gluten so finding a recipe for a gluten-free crust is a viable and easy option.

If you want to get wild you can even make it so your crust isn't bread at all! You can make a cauliflower base or even little zucchini pizzas. Your stone can cook anything you want and how you want it with the same result. Just make sure you keep an eye on the time!

Any power food can be spread on a pizza and so can any cheese. You're not limited to salty cured meats and dairy per se. Think outside the box and it will work. For example, what do you put in a salad? Kale, tomatoes, olives, peppers, pine nuts? They can all go on a pizza!

SECTION 4: MORE THAN PIZZA

BUT I DON'T WANT PIZZA TONIGHT

Though this book has pretty much proven the obsession most people have toward pizza, and rightfully so, the pizza stone can also be used for other types of cuisine!

At the beginning, I mentioned that the pizza stone is actually referred to as a baking stone. Essentially, it's merely a perfectly-designed piece of material made for heating food evenly throughout when you break it down. So, what else can you cook on the stone?

First off, just to clarify, you can put these foods directly on the stone – there is no reason for other pots and pans. Using the baking stone to roast your meals is a great use for it. You can roast a whole chicken or vegetables. Another great use for the baking stone is to bake bread! That's all pizza crust is, right? So why not make a nice loaf of sourdough for sandwiches or some soda bread for St. Paddy's.

The baking stone is so versatile that you'll end up using it a lot more than you would have ever imagined! In addition, you can also reheat your leftovers for a crisper, fresher taste than what you would find from a microwave. It's like you recooked it rather than reheated it!

Pizza is great, chicken and veggies are good, and bread is always a solid decision, but when it comes to baking, what actually comes to mind? Don't worry; no one will judge your answer. We all know you're thinking of dessert.

SWEET POSSIBILITIES

That's right, dessert. What's the big deal? We're trying to have fun here and add another skill to your resume. Trust me, people will appreciate the menu.

You can look at this two ways: First, you already ate pizza, you're feeling unhealthy, so you decide that it's your cheat day and you bake something gooey and delicious, or second, you made a really healthy pizza and you felt that your homemade creation deserves a reward and you have room for extra calories and some sugar. A win-win in my book… which you're reading.

How about an ice cream sandwich on a pizza stone? That doesn't make sense, I know, but baking the outside of the sandwich on the stone, taking the sides out, and putting some ice cream between is quite delicious – the heat and chill work perfectly because the baked part is cooked evenly throughout.

That's just one example. You can bake cookies, slab pies, brownies, and of course the classic giant chocolate chip cookie cake! It's okay, you can indulge. Oscar Wilde once said, "Everything in moderation, including moderation."

The pizza (or baking) stone is not just some one-use item that takes up space; it's a versatile piece that should become an essential part of your kitchen!

SECTION 5: SPECIAL CARE AND MAINTENANCE

RETURN THE FAVOR

Your pizza stone takes care of you, so you're going to have to take care of it. Some people may claim that a pizza stone may not have feelings like a human, and they may be right, but humans can certainly taste things that aren't very good and can get sick pretty easily if something isn't cleaned properly.

Pizza Stone- 1; Humans- 0.

Okay, I'll admit it, we have a lot more going for us than a stationary slab that resides in a hot box. Still though, to avoid a bad-tasting pizza or becoming ill, there are steps to make sure your stone is clean for the next go-around.

A pizza stone does require some special care, but it's not going to ruin your day or night. First of all, wait until the stone has completely cooled (I'm going to remind you of this again because for some reason I have to). Use a plastic scraper (similar to one you would use for your cast iron skillets) or a stiff dry brush and scrape with just enough force to remove any crumbs or burnt dough, cheese, or toppings. Next, wipe clear with a damp cloth and let air dry. It's really that simple.

Critical advice for the obsessive-compulsive: There may be a stain on your stone. Do not try and remove it with chemicals or soap. The stain will not affect the taste of your next pizza! Plus, it gives it a little character, and you won't be poisoned by your cleaning supplies.

Also, if there is something really caked onto the pizza stone (that isn't cake), you can use medium-grit sandpaper. Follow these steps and you will have your stone cleaned in no time and ready to be used again!

DON'T TOUCH THAT; IT'S HOT!

Cleaning seems as physically simple as it does mentally excruciating. With that being said, no one wants to wash dishes and other kitchen equipment unless they use the task as some sort of outlet for stress. If that's the case then feel free to wash away.

Because of this general attitude toward rinsing and scrubbing, some people may want to take the easy way out, tempted by the idea of being done when you're so close. I get it; it's hard to find the motivation after devouring a delicious pizza that you made. The couch or something entertaining is a much more appealing option.

When caring for your pizza stone, just remember these three things: don't touch it until it has completely cooled down (told you I would tell you again), don't wash with soap, and never submerge in water. Why? Well, you shouldn't touch hot things because it hurts and you should have learned that through trial and error as a child. If you use soap, the stone's pores will absorb it and your next dish will have a nice soapy bite to it if you're into gross things. Submerging the stone in water doesn't do much other than make it wet and harder to clean.

One final thing, if you plan to keep your stone in your oven, make sure it's out if you choose the self-cleaning cycle because the stone could crack during the process. There, I warned you! You have no excuses now so don't be lazy and just scrape away. It won't take long, and it's worth it for your next pizza creation!

SECTION 6: PRO TIPS

THE APPEAL OF A PEEL

So, you have your pizza in mind and then you prepare it. Now what? How the heck do you get your creation actually onto the stone?

You're going to need to get a pizza peel and it will make all the difference when it comes to prepping and transferring your pie to and from the stone. As like most things, you have options.

The pros use a metal peel. Roll out your dough on the counter, preferably marble or granite (though I know we're all not millionaires, so whatever is in your kitchen should be fine as long as the surface is clean). The metal peel will easily slide under the dough and your pizza won't stick to the counter, ruining the meal. If you're in the market, aluminum is the metal of choice.

Then there is the classic wooden pizza peels used to assemble your pie to avoid a sticky and messy counter. However, if it is a short-handle, you will still need to have a metal peel to transfer the pizza to and from the stone. Who has that kind of room in their kitchen? The people with marble or granite countertops probably. If you want to use a wooden peel and save some space, make sure it's a long-handled peel. This way you can assemble your pizza and transfer it, and the technique really limits the chance of a mishap.

That's great and all, but dough is still sticky! You need it to slide right onto the stone or the whole process is a disaster!

By: A.J. Luigi

NO PIZZA PEEL...NO PROBLEM!

Not every pizza stone comes equipped with a pizza peel. We do not want this to deter you from making any of the pizza recipes in this book. Have no fear. There are alternatives to the pizza peel.

For instance, you can use a stiff piece of cardboard. Make sure that the cardboard is big enough to hold the dressed pizza with one or two inches to spare. Sprinkle flour or cornmeal on the cardboard so that the dough does not stick to the cardboard at all.

If you don't feel like using a piece of cardboard or don't have one on hand, the back of a cookie sheet will also do. Sprinkle some cornmeal or flour on the back of the cookie sheet. Shake the pizza a little bit when you put it on the cookie sheet to ensure that it doesn't stick. You can try running a piece of string or floss underneath the crust to keep it from sticking, as well.

Be cautious when you remove the pizza off of the stone. Use a pair of tongs to catch the pizza at the rim and put it back on the piece of cardboard, cookie sheet or a large plate. Then let it cool before eating.

NATURAL ASSISTANCE

Listen, making pizza isn't the most tidy of processes. Even the pros know that. In other words, your kitchen and counters are going to get a little messy and you need to be okay with that. It's fun!

There are three main choices for helping the pizza slide off the peel and onto your stone: corn meal, rice flour, or regular flour.

My go-to is cornmeal; it still amazes me how it works. I prefer it because it makes the uncooked dough slide right onto and off the peel then onto and off the stone without any hassle whatsoever. However, the main downside is that it really gets everywhere, and no matter how much you clean, a few days later you will see some cornmeal somewhere. Another issue, and this depends on the person, is not everyone likes the taste and texture of cornmeal and would prefer another alternative.

Rice flour also works very well if you don't want your pizza to stick to the counter or peel, but again, preferences come into play with such a unique assistant. If you want to go traditional Italian and bet on a sure thing, then use regular flour. It will prevent sticking and you and your guests won't mind the taste... and if they complain then you shouldn't invite them over anymore because they obviously don't like pizza.

ONE LAST THING

You mean this isn't over yet? Come on, man! I want to use my pizza stone already!

Okay, okay, calm down. My last piece of advice is that if you choose to store your stone in the oven (which is very common; I do it) then make sure you take it out while cooking other meals that don't require its use. It will just take the oven to heat up longer if the pizza stone is hogging all the heat.

But for pizza, let the pizza stone do its thing! Now go and get your hands dirty and enjoy delicious, masonry-oven, restaurant-style pizza at home!

By: A.J. Luigi

BEFORE YOU GO FURTHER...

GET YOUR QUICK START GRILLING GUIDE

EASY AS 1 - 2 - 3

A SIMPLE STEP GUIDE FOR MAKING PIZZA STONE PIZZA ON THE GRILL!

Learn the basics when grilling your stone! This quick start guide will show you the proper way to get your pizza stone on the grill and baking your pizzas in no time! **Get yours NOW** by just simply clicking the button below! Hope you enjoy!

http://eepurl.com/dsZ_NP

SECTION 7:
THE CRUST, THE WHOLE CRUST, &
NOTHING BUT THE CRUST:

Ask any Italian pie maker, pizza crust is more than just bread. It is the foundation of the pizza itself. A burnt, lifeless crust will kill the taste and flavor of the pizza. This is why so many different chefs perfect the way they make their crust because without it there is no pizza.

There are a lot of different ways to make dough, especially when it comes to the type of consistency that you want to achieve: traditional, pan, thin crust or even deep dish. However, the world of pizza has grown and there are so many alternative ways to make crust nowadays.

For instance, those who have gluten allergies don't have to sit this one out. You are allowed to eat pizza again: from gluten free flour, to cauliflower, zucchini or squash. You can eat your pizza and not have to worry about the guilt either. Either way you look at it, if you just want to be healthy, have a food allergy or want to try something different. Our crust section has something for everyone to enjoy.

RISING PIZZA DOUGH

Nothing is better than pizza! However, we all know that the best part of pizza is the dough! Learning how to create and perfect your dough is what is going to make your homemade pizza a success.

Total Time: 85 minutes
Makes: 6 Servings

INGREDIENTS:

Makes enough for two 10-12 inch pizzas
1 ½ cups warm water
1 package active dry yeast
3 ¾ cups bread flour
2 tbsp. olive oil
2 tsp. salt
1 tsp. sugar

DIRECTIONS:

> Equipment needed: Pizza Stone, peel and brush (for oil)
> Preheat oven to 475 and place the pizza stone in the oven.
> Pour warm water in the bowl of a standing mixer.
> Lightly pour the yeast in the water and let sit for 5 minutes, make sure the yeast has fully dissolved in the water.
> Mix in the flour, salt, sugar, and olive oil. Using the mixing paddle, place the setting on low speed for 1 minute.
> Replace the paddle with the dough hook attachment and knead the pizza dough on low for 8 minutes.
> Sprinkle olive oil in a large bowl and coat the dough with the oil. Cover the dough with plastic wrap and set in a warm setting for no less than 1 ½ hours.
> Punch the dough down to release the air.

> Separate the dough into two and roll each half into a ball.
> Let rest into two separate bowls, lightly covered for 15 minutes
> Sprinkle the peel with cornmeal
> Flatten the dough on the peel to make a 12-inch-wide circle.
> Lift the dough to create a lip at the edges
> Brush the top lightly with olive oil.
> With your fingers push dents into the surface to prevent bubbling.
> Start prepping for your pizza creation
> Now go to the TOC for your choice of Sauce **(pg. 44)** and Toppings **(pg. 69)**

THIN CRUST PIZZA CRUST

When eating pizza, we want the ingredients to stand out. Making a really thin crust lets you have that freedom.

Total Time: 85 minutes
Makes: 4 Servings

INGREDIENTS:
Makes enough for two 10-12 inch pizzas
¾ cup lukewarm water
1 tsp. active dry yeast
2 cups unbleached all-purpose flour
¾ tsp. salt
2 tsp. olive oil, divided

DIRECTIONS:
> Equipment needed: Pizza Stone, peel, and brush (for olive oil)
> Preheat oven to 475 and place the pizza stone in the oven.
> Pour warm water in the bowl of a standing mixer.
> Lightly pour the yeast in the water and let sit for 5 minutes, make sure the yeast has fully dissolved in the water.
> Mix in the flour, and salt. Using the mixing paddle, place the setting on low speed for 1 minute.
> Replace the paddle with the dough hook attachment and knead the pizza dough on low for 8 minutes.
> Sprinkle olive oil in a large bowl and coat the dough with the oil. Cover the dough with plastic wrap and set in a warm setting for no less than 1 ½ hours.
> Punch the dough down to release the air.
> Separate the dough into two and roll each half into a ball.

- ❯ Let rest into two separate bowls, lightly covered for 15 minutes
- ❯ Sprinkle the peel with cornmeal
- ❯ Flatten the dough on the peel to make a 12-inch-wide circle.
- ❯ Use the heel of your hand, gently press down and stretch the dough until it is ¼ inch thick or less
- ❯ Lift the dough to create a lip at the edges
- ❯ Brush the top lightly with olive oil.
- ❯ With your fingers push dents into the surface to prevent bubbling.
- ❯ Cook for 8-12 minutes.
- ❯ Start prepping for your pizza creation
- ❯ Now go to the TOC for your choice of Sauce **(pg. 44)** and Toppings **(pg. 69)**

CRACKER PIZZA CRUST

This crispy, flaky, crackly and great for the belly crust give you the chance to eat 7 more slices if you wanted to. And the best part is that the no yeast and no rise recipe makes it easier to make without compromising on the texture and flavor.

Total Time: 85 minutes

Makes: 24 Servings

INGREDIENTS:

5 tbsp. warm water
2 tsp. olive oil, divided
¼ tsp. active dry yeast
3.5 ounces bread flour
3.5 ounces bread flour
3 tbsp. semolina flour
2 tbsp. fresh rosemary, chopped
½ tsp. salt

DIRECTIONS:

> Equipment needed: Pizza Stone, peel, measuring cup, and brush (for oil)
> Preheat oven to 475 and place the pizza stone in the oven.
> Combine water, 1 tbsp. oil and yeast in a bowl. Let stand for 2 minutes.
> Weigh out 5 oz. bread crumbs in a measuring cup.
> Sprinkle over the yeast mixture, add the rosemary, semolina flour and salt.
> Stir together until combined.
> Knead dough on counter for 1 minutes
> Sprinkle 1 tbsp. olive oil in a large bowl and coat the dough with the oil. Cover the dough with plastic wrap and set in a warm setting for 40 minutes.
> Sprinkle the peel with cornmeal
> Flatten the dough on the peel to make a 12-inch-wide circle.
> Brush the top lightly with olive oil.
> Cook for 5 minutes. Start prepping for your pizza creation
> Now go to the TOC for your choice of Sauce **(pg. 44)** and Toppings **(pg. 69)**

ST. LOUIS SYTLE PIZZA CRUST

The St. Louis Style Pizza is the King of the Cracker pizza crust. Yet, we don't want you to stop there. Once you make this crust you will want to know how to make the rest of the recipe.

Total Time: 15 minutes

Makes: 12 Servings

INGREDIENTS:

Makes enough for two 10-12 inch pizzas
2 cups all-purpose flour
2 tbsp. all-purpose flour
½ tsp. salt
1 tsp. baking powder
2 tsp. olive oil
2 tsp. dark corn syrup
½ cup water
2 tbsp. water

DIRECTIONS:

> Equipment needed: Pizza Stone, peel, brush (for oil)
> Preheat oven to 475 and place the pizza stone in the oven.
> Mix all of the ingredients together in a bowl.
> Separate the dough into two and roll each half into a ball.
> Sprinkle the peel with cornmeal
> Flatten the dough on the peel paper thin to make a 12-inch-wide circle.
> Brush the top lightly with olive oil.
> With your fingers push dents into the surface to prevent bubbling.
> Cook for 15 minutes.
> Start prepping for your pizza creation
> Now go to the TOC for your choice of Sauce **(pg. 44)** and Toppings **(pg. 69)**

SECTION 8:
HEALTHIER PIZZA CRUSTS:

Some of us feel guilty when the thought of pizza fills our minds. Or the fact that you are allergic to gluten makes you feel iffy when you think of pizza. Either way, there are healthier versions of dough that you can eat that will not make you feel guilty or mess with your allergies. We have added some of the recipes right here in this section.

When making pizza dough, there is an option to replace the white flour with another type of flour to fit your needs. For instance, you can substitute whole wheat flour, oat flour, beans (black beans or chickpeas), buckwheat flour, nut flours, spelt flour, and coconut flour to name a few.

If you have a gluten allergy finding gluten and wheat free flour is not as big as a challenge as you think. Here are a few options you can choose to replace regular flour: amaranth flour, arrowroot flour, banana flour, barley flour, brown rice flour, buckwheat flour, chia flour, chickpea flour, coconut flour, Coffee flour, corn flour, cornmeal, hemp flour, lupine flour, maize flour, millet flour, oat flour, potato flour, potato starch flour, quinoa flour, rye flour (wheat free), sorghum flour, soya flour, tapioca flour, teff flour, and white rice flour to name a few.

Choose any of these flours to substitute regular wheat flour in making your pizza crusts or choose some of the recipes we have added below.

CALIFLOWER CRUST

Cauliflower is a great food source that contains 77 percent of the recommended daily value of Vitamin C in one serving. Who knew that eating pizza could be so healthy for you?

Total Time: 60 minutes

Makes: 6 Servings

INGREDIENTS:

1 small head of cauliflower, chopped
1 cup Parmesan cheese, grated
¾ tsp. Italian Seasoning
1 garlic clove, minced
½ tsp. salt
½ tsp. pepper
1 egg

DIRECTIONS:

> Equipment needed: Pizza Stone, peel, parchment paper, and brush (for oil)
> Preheat oven to 475 and place the pizza stone in the oven.
> Pour the chopped cauliflower in a food processor and mix until finely ground.
> Cook cauliflower in a microwave safe bowl for approximately 4-5 min.
> Pour the cauliflower onto a towel and squeeze out all of the liquid.
> Add the cauliflower, Parmesan, Italian Seasoning, garlic, salt, pepper and the egg to a large bowl. Mix together until the mixture holds together.
> Line the pizza peel with parchment paper and brush with olive oil.
> Spread the mixture onto the peel until if forms a 12-inch-wide circle.
> Slide the parchment paper onto the pizza stone.
> Bake for 15 minutes until the crust is slightly golden.
> Now go to the TOC for your choice of Sauce **(pg. 44)** and Toppings **(pg. 69)**

ZUCCHINI CRUST

Zucchini is great in spaghetti and even in place of noodles. But, who would have thought to make a crust out of it. This universal vegetable packs a crunch and a punch in your mouth that will have you use this ingredient for your crust anytime.

Total Time: 45 minutes
Makes: 6 Servings

INGREDIENTS:

2 cups shredded zucchini, dried
2 large eggs, lightly beaten
¼ cup all-purpose flour
¼ tsp. salt
1/4 cup Parmesan cheese
½ cup Mozzarella cheese
1 tbsp. olive oil

DIRECTIONS:

❯ Equipment needed: Pizza Stone, peel, parchment paper, and brush (for oil)
❯ Preheat oven to 475 and place the pizza stone in the oven.
❯ Combine all ingredients into a large bowl
❯ Line the pizza peel with parchment paper and brush with olive oil.
❯ Spread the mixture onto the peel until if forms a 12-inch-wide circle.
❯ Slide the parchment paper onto the pizza stone.
❯ Bake for 15 minutes until the crust is slightly golden.
❯ Now go to the TOC for your choice of Sauce **(pg. 44)** and Toppings **(pg. 69)**

BUTTERNUT SQUASH CRUST

This grain free pizza crust gives your pizza a sweet and creamy flavor that you cannot get with cauliflower. So, just pick your toppings and have fun with it.

Total Time: 67 minutes
Makes: 4 Servings

INGREDIENTS:

1 ½ cups butternut squash, mashed
½ cups all-purpose flour
½ cup shredded Mozzarella cheese
1 tbsp. Parmesan cheese
½ tsp. fresh sage, minced
½ tsp. baking powder
½ tsp. salt
¼ tsp. granulated garlic
1 pinch nutmeg
1 pinch cayenne pepper
1 egg, beaten
1 tbsp. olive oil

DIRECTIONS:

> Equipment needed: Pizza Stone, peel, parchment paper, and brush (for oil)
> Preheat oven to 475 and place the pizza stone in the oven.
> Pour all of the ingredients into a large bowl.
> Line the pizza peel with parchment paper and brush with olive oil.
> Spread the mixture onto the peel until if forms a 12-inch-wide circle.
> Slide the parchment paper onto the pizza stone.
> Bake for 25 minutes until the crust is slightly golden, flip and bake for 15 minutes more.
> Now go to the TOC for your choice of Sauce **(pg. 44)** and Toppings **(pg. 69)**.

WHOLE-WHEAT DOUGH

There tends to be a bad rap when it comes to whole- wheat anything. Sometimes it can be flavorless and tough. But, we guarantee that this recipe will have you wondering if you used regular flour instead.

Total Time: 15 minutes

Makes: 4 Servings

INGREDIENTS:

¾ cup whole-wheat flour
¾ cup all-purpose flour
1 package quick rising yeast
¾ tsp. salt
¼ tsp. sugar
2/3 cup hot water
2 tsp. extra-virgin olive oil

DIRECTIONS:

> Equipment needed: Pizza Stone, peel, and brush (for oil)
> Preheat oven to 475 and place the pizza stone in the oven.
> Combine flour, yeast, salt and sugar in a food processor.
> Combine the hot water and oil in a measuring cup and gradually pour in the liquid while the mixture is pulsing.
> Sprinkle olive oil in a large bowl and coat the dough with the oil. Cover the dough with plastic wrap and set in a warm setting for no less than 1 ½ hrs.
> Punch the dough down to release the air.
> Sprinkle the peel with cornmeal
> Flatten the dough on the peel to make a 12-inch-wide circle.
> Lift the dough to create a lip at the edges
> Brush the top lightly with olive oil.
> With your fingers push dents into the surface to prevent bubbling.
> Now go to the TOC for your choice of Sauce **(pg. 44)** and Toppings **(pg. 69)**

FLATBREAD (GLUTEN FREE) PIZZA CRUST

Flatbread gives the exotic feel to the pizza. It is soft, flaky, and can be cut into squares. But, above all, it is gluten free.

Total Time: 20 minutes

Makes: 8 Servings

INGREDIENTS:

Makes enough for two 10-12 inch pizzas
1 cup tapioca flour
½ cup coconut flour
¼ tsp. salt
½ cup canned coconut milk
¼ cup butter
¼ cup water
3 garlic cloves, minced
1 egg

DIRECTIONS:

> Equipment needed: Pizza Stone and peel
> Preheat oven to 475 and place the pizza stone in the oven.
> Mix the tapioca and coconut flour and salt together in a medium bowl.
> Using a small pot, heat the coconut milk, butter, water and garlic over medium high until it simmers.
> Mixt the hot and dry ingredients together.
> Let cool
> Whisk the egg and add to the mixture.
> Let sit for 5 minutes.
> Sprinkle the peel with cornmeal
> Spread the dough thinly on the peel to make a 12-inch-wide circle.
> Bake for 7 minutes.
> Now go to the TOC for your choice of Sauce **(pg. 44)** and Toppings **(pg. 69)**

BEET STYLE PIZZA CRUST

Beets usually have a very strong flavor, but you cannot taste them in the crust. The best thing about the crust, besides it being good for you, is the fact that it is so colorful. It can be great eye candy for your next event.

Total Time: 30 minutes

Makes: 8 Servings

INGREDIENTS:

Makes enough for two 10-12 inch pizzas
1 cup warm water
2 tsp dry active yeast
3 cups flour
2 tsp. salt
2 tsp. honey
¾ cup beet, cooked and pureed

DIRECTIONS:

> Equipment needed: Pizza Stone and peel
> Preheat oven to 475 and place the pizza stone in the oven.
> Mix the water and yeast together.
> Add flour, honey, and beets to the mixture.
> Knead the dough on a countertop until it is mixed well.
> Form into a ball and oil a bowl. Place inside the bowl and cover with wrap.
> Let sit for 2 hours.
> Divide the dough into two separate crusts and can refrigerate one for later.
> Sprinkle the peel with cornmeal
> Spread the dough thinly on the peel to make a 12-inch-wide circle.
> Bake for 7 minutes.
> Now go to the TOC for your choice of Sauce **(pg. 44)** and Toppings **(pg. 69)**

EGGPLANT PIZZA CRUST

This low-carb, earthy crust is going to make you love this pizza even more. Deliciousness is something we do not compromise here, just the carbs.

Total Time: 20 minutes

Makes: 3 Servings

INGREDIENTS:

1 large eggplant, cut into ¼ inch slices
1 ½ tsp. salt
6 oz. Parmesan Cheese
1 ½ tsp. extra-virgin olive oil
1 garlic clove, minced

DIRECTIONS:

> Equipment needed: Pizza Stone, 2 baking sheets, parchment paper, and brush (for oil)
> Preheat oven to 425 and place the pizza stone in the oven.
> Line baking sheet with paper towels.
> Place each of the eggplant slices in one layer on baking sheet.
> Sprinkle each piece with salt and let sit for 15 minutes.
> Pat the eggplant dry.
> Add parchment paper to another baking sheet and arrange the eggplant in a circular pattern.
> Sprinkle with 1 cup Parmesan cheese.
> Brush with olive oil
> Transfer to the pizza stone and cook for 15 minutes.
> Now go to the TOC for your choice of Sauce **(pg. 44)** and Toppings **(pg. 69)**

SWEET POTATO PIZZA CRUST

Sweet potatoes are so versatile that we had to make a pizza crust out of them. When cooking the crust, you are going to love the color, the aroma of the spices and the puffiness of the crust. It is going to knock you out of this world.

Total Time: 50 minutes
Makes: 8 Servings

INGREDIENTS:

3 sweet potatoes, medium
1 cup almond flour
1 egg
½ tsp. salt
1 tsp. dried oregano
1 tsp. dried basil
1 tsp. garlic powder
1 tbsp. apple cider vinegar

DIRECTIONS:

> Equipment needed: Pizza Stone and peel
> Preheat oven to 400 and place the pizza stone in the oven.
> Cook the potatoes in the microwave until soft.
> Peel and add to large mixing bowl with flour, egg, salt, dried oregano, basil, garlic powder and apple cider vinegar.
> Mash until combined.
> Mix the tapioca and coconut flour and salt together in a medium bowl.
> Using a small pot, heat the coconut milk, butter, water and garlic over medium high until it simmers.Sprinkle the peel with cornmeal
> Spread the dough thinly on the peel to make a 12-inch-wide circle.
> Bake for 30 minutes.
> Now go to the TOC for your choice of Sauce **(pg. 44)** and Toppings **(pg. 69)**

SECTION 9:
LET'S GET SAUCY / WHICH TO
CHOOSE:

Let's get saucy everyone! We know that everyone loves pizza and the sauce can make or break the pizza. If you do not combine the right sauce with the correct toppings, your pizza is going to taste a little off. This particular section will help you decide what sauce goes great with the type of toppings you want to put on your pizza.

We have engineered a sauce recipe for everyone in this section. For those who are allergic to tomatoes, we have an alternative variety that will make your mouth water in ways you would have never imagined. The Savory Pumpkin Puree Sauce or No Tomatoes in this Tomato Sauce are made with pumpkin puree and beets, which give the sauce a great color, but your taste buds, will never know that you are not eating tomatoes at all.

This section also provides many different types of sauces for those who want to try something new. From creamy Alfredo to nutty pesto or from zesty salsa to Greek style hummus, this section has a type of sauce that everyone will enjoy.

PINE NUTTY PESTO SAUCE

Pesto sauce is the nutty alternative to tomato sauce. Spread it on your pizza dough and see what will go with its nutty flavor

Total Time: 15 minutes
Makes: 1 cup

INGREDIENTS:

2 cups fresh basil leaves
½ cup Parmesan cheese, grated
½ cup extra virgin olive oil
1/3 cup pine nuts
3 garlic cloves, minced
½ tsp. Salt
½ tsp. Pepper

DIRECTIONS:

> Equipment needed: Food processor
> Pour the basil and pine nuts in the food processor
> Pulse several times
> Next, add in the garlic and cheese.
> Pulse several times
> Scrape the sides with a spatula
> While running, stir in the olive oil
> Do not let it separate
> Stir in the salt and pepper to taste
> Start prepping for your pizza creation
> Now go to the TOC for your selection of Pizza Toppings **(pg. 69)**

CREAMY BECHAMEL SAUCE

If you're tired of the traditional pizza – Have no Fear! This white sauce will add a little creaminess to your pie.

Total Time: 15 minutes
Makes: 2 cups

INGREDIENTS:

¼ cup butter
1/3 cup flour, plain
2 cups milk
1 ¼ cheddar cheese, grated
3 tbsp. Parmesan cheese, grated
½ tsp. Nutmeg
½ tsp. Salt
½ tsp. Pepper

DIRECTIONS:

> Pour the butter in a saucepan and melt over low heat
> Next, add the flour and whisk until the mixture is smooth
> Cook for 2 minutes
> Gradually stir in the milk to avoid lumps
> Add the salt, pepper and nutmeg.
> Cook for 7 minutes. Remember to stir frequently to thicken the sauce.
> Remove when it comes to a boil.
> Stir in the cheese and
> Start prepping for your pizza creation
> Now go to the TOC for your selection of Pizza Toppings **(pg. 69)**

ZESTY SALSA RECIPE

Salsa is one of the most universal foods. Is it an appetizer? Is it a sauce? You be the judge.

Total Time: 10 minutes
Makes: 2 cups

INGREDIENTS:

1 medium lime, juice
10 Roma tomatoes
½ cup cilantro, fresh
1 garlic clove
¼ of a medium red onion, chopped
1 jalapeno
1 tbsp. olive oil
½ tsp. Salt

DIRECTIONS:

> Equipment needed: food processor
> Pour all of the ingredients into a food processor. Pulse until well mixed, but chunky.
> Salt to taste
> For a thicker sauce, strain some of the liquid.
> Start prepping for your pizza creation
> Now go to the TOC for your selection of Pizza Toppings **(pg. 69)**

SWEET AND TANGY BARBEQUE SAUCE

Barbeque sauce is great slathered on anything. Why would your pizza be any different? Combine the two together and you will not be disappointed.

Total Time: 25 minutes
Makes: 2 cups

INGREDIENTS:
1 tbsp. olive oil
½ small onion, chopped
1 garlic clove, chopped
1 cup ketchup
¼ cup apple cider vinegar
¼ cup molasses
2 tbsp. brown sugar
2 tbsp. Dijon mustard
2 tsp. Worcestershire sauce
1 tbsp. chili powder
¼ tsp. cayenne pepper
¾ cup water
½ tsp. Salt
½ tsp. Pepper

DIRECTIONS:
> Pour the oil in a medium saucepan and heat.
> Add in the onion, and garlic.
> Cook for 5 minutes and stir frequently.
> Next, add the rest of the ingredients and let simmer for 15 minutes until it thickens.
> Sir frequently
> Start prepping for your pizza creation
> Now go to the TOC for your selection of Pizza Toppings **(pg. 69)**

SAVORY PUMPKIN PUREE SAUCE

Pumpkin on a pizza? This is a great alternative for those who can't eat tomatoes because of their acidity. Try this sauce and you won't even notice the difference.

Total Time: 15 minutes
Makes: 2 cups

INGREDIENTS:

2 cups pumpkin puree
2 cup tomato sauce
1 garlic cloves, minced
1 tsp. Italian seasoning

DIRECTIONS:

> Mix all of the ingredients in a saucepan.

> Simmer for 15 minutes on medium heat.

> Stir frequently.

> Add more seasoning if desired.

> Start prepping for your pizza creation

> Now go to the TOC for your selection of Pizza Toppings **(pg. 69)**

HUM FOR HUMMUS STYLE PIZZA SAUCE

Hummus – the Greek Salsa – is a great healthy way to jazz up your pizza. Add some onion, peppers, olives and feta cheese to your pizza.

Total Time: 5 minutes
Makes: 3 cups

INGREDIENTS:

2/3 cup of tahini, roasted
¼ cup extra virgin olive oil
2 garlic cloves, mashed
1 25-oz cans of garbanzo beans, drained
¼ cup lemon juice, freshly squeezed
½ cup water
½ cup salt
Garnish: paprika, olive oil, toasted pine nuts, chopped parsley

DIRECTIONS:

> Equipment needed: Food Processor
> Pour the tahini and olive oil in a food processor and pulse smoothly.
> Next, add the garlic, garbanzo beans, lemon juice, water and salt in the food processor.
> Mix until smooth.
> Add more salt and lemon juice to taste.
> Start prepping for your pizza creation
> Now go to the TOC for your selection of Pizza Toppings **(pg. 69)**

NO TOMATO IN THIS TOMATO SAUCE

Combining beets and pumpkin together makes for a great sauce. The beets are both sweet and add a great color to the sauce. Pair some garlic and basil and you will love this change to the norm.

Total Time: 45 minutes
Makes: 4 cups

INGREDIENTS:

3 tbsp. olive oil
1 medium red onion, chopped
½ tsp. thyme, dried
5 garlic cloves, minced
1 ½ cup carrots, sliced into coins
3 tbsp. lemon juice, freshly squeezed
1 tbsp. balsamic vinegar
2 cups pumpkin puree
1 package peeled and ready to eat beets
½ tsp. Salt
½ tsp. Pepper

DIRECTIONS:

> Pour the olive oil in a skillet and heat.
> Sauté the onion and thyme for 10 minutes. Stir often.
> Add the garlic and sauté for 1 minute
> Next, add the carrots, lemon juice, balsamic vinegar, salt and pepper and water to cover the carrots
> Let the ingredients come to a boil.
> Lower the heat, cover and simmer for 30 minutes
> While the carrots are cooking, add the beets and the pumpkin puree to a blender.
> Mix until smooth

> When carrots are done cooking, scoop into the blender and blend with the pumpkin mixture.
> Start prepping for your pizza creation
> Now go to the TOC for your selection of Pizza Toppings **(pg. 69)**

BLACK OLIVE TAPENADE SAUCE

Olives and pizza go together like peanut butter and jelly. Spread it thickly on your dough, with some grilled vegetables.

Total Time: 6 minutes
Makes: 1 cup

INGREDIENTS:

7 oz. black olives, pitted
1 garlic clove, minced
3 anchovies
8 small capers
2 tbsp. olive oil, divided

DIRECTIONS:

> Equipment needed: Food Processor
> Pour olives, garlic, anchovies, capers and 1 tbsp. olive oil in the food processor
> Mix for 15 seconds
> Scrape down the edges with a spatula
> Add the other tbsp. of olive oil
> Process for 30 seconds until smooth.
> Make sure there are no garlic chunks left
> Start prepping for your pizza creation
> Now go to the TOC for your selection of Pizza Toppings **(pg. 69)**

CARROT CHILI PASTE SAUCE

A North African chili paste will show you a whole new way to eat pizza. Let us start thinking outside the box.

Total Time: 20 minutes
Makes: 3 1/2 cups

INGREDIENTS:

2 cups vegetable broth
1 lb. carrots, peeled and coarsely chopped
2 medium garlic cloves
1 15 oz. can garbanzo beans, drained
4 tbsp. extra virgin olive oil
3 tbsp. almond butter
5 large ice cubes
4 tbsp. harissa paste
2 tbsp. lemon juiced, freshly squeezed
1 tbsp. honey
½ tsp. Salt
½ tsp. Pepper

DIRECTIONS:

> Pour the vegetable broth in a small saucepan.
> Bring to boil over high heat.
> Next, add the garlic and carrots.
> Reduce to medium and cook for 10 minutes,
> Remove from the stove and let cool.
> Place the carrots, garlic, 1 ½ cups cooking liquid and the garbanzo beans in a food processor
> Mix until smooth.
> Add the olive oil, almond butter and ice cubes with the mixture.
> Pulse until smooth

> Mix in 3 tbsp. of the harissa, lemon juice, honey, salt and pepper and pulse.
> Taste and add more seasoning as desired.
> Start prepping for your pizza creation
> Now go to the TOC for your selection of Pizza Toppings **(pg. 69)**

GARLIC AND OLIVE OIL SAUCE

When you are mincing up the garlic, remember not to overdo it. Rub this sauce on your dough and then add some light toppings for a more refined type of pizza pie.

Total Time: 5 minutes

Makes: 2 cups

INGREDIENTS:

½ cup extra virgin olive oil
6 large garlic cloves, peeled
¼ cup parsley leaves, minced
¼ tsp Salt
½ tsp. Pepper

DIRECTIONS:

> Pour first four ingredients into a small skillet
> Cook for 5 minutes on medium-low
> Stir often
> Remove from the stove
> Stir in parsley and pepper
> Start prepping for your pizza creation
> Now go to the TOC for your selection of Pizza Toppings **(pg. 69)**

PEPPERY JELLY PIZZA STYLE SAUCE

If you're tired of the traditional cheese pizza – Try pepper jelly. This will give your pizza a unique flavor that you will run to every time you want to eat something out of the norm.

Total Time: 15 minutes
Makes: 2 cups

INGREDIENTS:

1 jar Smucker's apple jelly
5 medium jalapenos, chopped
1 tsp. red pepper flakes
½ tsp. garlic powder
½ tsp. tabasco
½ tsp. black pepper

DIRECTIONS:

- ❯ Pour the jelly in a saucepan and warm over low heat
- ❯ Make sure that it becomes a liquid like consistency
- ❯ Mix in the other ingredients and mix well
- ❯ Put ingredients back in the jar
- ❯ Put in fridge
- ❯ Take out every 30 minutes and shake until peppers evenly distribute throughout the jelly
- ❯ Start prepping for your pizza creation
- ❯ Now go to the TOC for your selection of Pizza Toppings **(pg. 69)**

MISO AND MACADAMIAN NUT RICOTTA SAUCE

Ricotta cheese is the cream cheese of Italian cuisine. When creating your pie, spread a thin layer and even add basil, grilled vegetables, tomatoes and even lemon to give you pizza a taste to remember.

Total Time: 5 minutes
Makes: 2 cups

INGREDIENTS:

1 ½ cups macadamia nuts
3 tbsp. lemon juice
1 tbsp. nutritional yeast
1 tbsp. white miso paste
1 garlic clove
¼ cup water

DIRECTIONS:

> Equipment needed: food processor
> Pour the macadamia nuts, lemon juice, yeast, miso paste, garlic and water into the food processor
> Blend until smooth and has a creamy texture
> Scrape down the sides with a spatula.
> Add 1 tsp. of water if needed until the ricotta texture is reached
> Start prepping for your pizza creation
> Now go to the TOC for your selection of Pizza Toppings **(pg. 69)**

CARAMELIZED ONION SAUCE

Caramelized onions are a savory treat. When topping your pizza remember to compliment the sauce with some feta cheese, mushrooms, arugula, prosciutto and balsamic vinegar.

Total Time: 35 minutes
Makes: 2 cups

INGREDIENTS:

1 tbsp. butter
3 cups onion, thinly sliced
1 cup red wine, dry
3 cups low sodium chicken broth
1/8 tsp. salt
1/8 tsp. black pepper

DIRECTIONS:

> Pour the butter into a large skillet and melt over medium heat
> Mix in the onion
> Cook for 5 minutes and stir frequently
> Continue to cook for 15 minutes
> Add the wine and cook for 5 more minutes
> Remove the onion from the pan and finely chop
> Return to pan
> Add in the broth, salt and pepper and stir
> Let it come to a boil
> And cook for 10 minutes until it is reduced to 2 cups
> Start prepping for your pizza creation
> Now go to the TOC for your selection of Pizza Toppings **(pg. 69)**

GO BACK TO THE BASICS TOMATO SAUCE

There is nothing wrong with going back to the basics and spreading your pie with tomato sauce. Sometimes it's good to go back to what made us fall in love with pizza in the first place.

Total Time: 15 minutes
Makes: 2 cups

INGREDIENTS:
1 tbsp. olive oil
2 garlic cloves, minced
¼ cup red wine
1 28- oz. can crushed tomatoes
1 small can tomato paste
1 tbsp. sugar
1 tsp. Italian seasoning
½ tsp. Salt
½ tsp. Pepper

DIRECTIONS:
> Pour the oil in a medium saucepan
> Add the garlic
> Sauté over high heat for 1 minute
> Pour in the wine and simmer for 2 minutes
> Add the remaining ingredients and heat through.
> Taste and add seasonings if needed
> Start prepping for your pizza creation
> Now go to the TOC for your selection of Pizza Toppings **(pg. 69)**

MIDDLE EASTERN ZAATAR SAUCE

This Middle Eastern sauce makes for a great alternative for what you are used to. Pair it with tomatoes, feta, olives and even mint. See how that tastes on your palate.

Total Time: 8 minutes
Makes: 2 cups

INGREDIENTS:

3 tbsp. sesame seeds
3 tbsp. thyme leaves, thyme
1 tbsp. sumac powder
2/3 tsp. salt

DIRECTIONS:

> Pour the sesame seeds in dry skillet over medium heat
> Toast for 5 minutes
> Next, combine the seeds, thyme leaves, sumac and salt in a bowl
> Stir well
> Start prepping for your pizza creation
> Now go to the TOC for your selection of Pizza Toppings **(pg. 69)**

THAI PEANUT SAUCE

Turn your pizza into a Thai dish. By adding bean sprouts, scallions, chicken, and ginger over your sauce you will have created a successful Thai-themed pizza.

Total Time: 8 minutes
Makes: 2 cups

INGREDIENTS:

1 14 oz. can coconut milk
3 tbsp. red curry paste
1 cup natural creamy peanut butter, unsweetened
3 tbsp. low sodium soy sauce
¼ cup honey
2 tbsp. rice vinegar
½ cup water
½ tsp. sesame oil

DIRECTIONS:

> Pour all the ingredients in a saucepan and bring to a simmer.
> Cook for 3 minutes
> Stir often
> Let the sauce cool.
> Start prepping for your pizza creation
> Now go to the TOC for your selection of Pizza Toppings **(pg. 69)**

JAPANESE LIME WASABI SAUCE

For those who want to try something different and spicy, this is the sauce for you. Add some ahi tuna or some crab meat and avocado with a sprinkle of soy sauce and you will have a sushi-themed pizza.

Total Time: 10 minutes
Makes: 1 cup

INGREDIENTS:

2 tbsp. lime juice, fresh
2 tbsp. wasabi sauce
1 tbsp. fresh ginger, minced
1 tbsp. rice vinegar
¼ tsp. salt
1/8 tsp. black pepper
½ cup olive oil

DIRECTIONS:

> Pour first six ingredients into a small bowl
> Stir in the olive oil
> Let rest
> Start prepping for your pizza creation
> Now go to the TOC for your selection of Pizza Toppings **(pg. 69)**

GARLIC AIOLI PIZZA SAUCE

Garlic Aioli is great paired with seafood and vegetables. Make a shrimp or tuna topped pizza with tomatoes and basil. You will have yourself a hit.

Total Time: 65 minutes
Makes: 2 cups

INGREDIENTS:

1 cup mayonnaise
3 garlic cloves, minced
1 tbsp. lemon juice
1 pinch cayenne pepper

DIRECTIONS:

> Pour all of the ingredients into a small bowl
> Stir together
> Cover with plastic wrap
> Refrigerate for 1 hour
> Start prepping for your pizza creation
> Now go to the TOC for your selection of Pizza Toppings **(pg. 69)**

BASIL AND SUN-DRIED TOMATO SAUCE

This is a sauce that will pair well with pepperoni and olive pizza. The flavors pack a punch that is simple, which is what we want from our ingredients.

Total Time: 20 minutes
Makes: 2 cups

INGREDIENTS:

2 tbsp. extra virgin olive oil
1 whole yellow onion, diced
3 garlic cloves, minced
3 whole sun-dried tomatoes packed in oil, drained and chopped
½ cup white wine, dry
1 can fire roasted tomatoes
1 can tomato sauce
1 tbsp. oregano, dried
2 tbsp. fresh basil, chopped
½ tsp. Salt
½ tsp. Pepper

DIRECTIONS:

> Pour the oil in a medium saucepan
> Heat over medium heat
> Add in the onion and sauté for 5 minutes
> Next, add in the garlic and sun-dried tomatoes
> Sauté for 2 minutes
> Remember not to burn the garlic
> Deglaze the pan with wine
> Simmer for 2 minutes
> Stir in tomatoes and tomato sauce
> Reduce the heat to medium low
> Stir in the oregano and basil

> Season with salt and pepper
> Simmer for 15 minutes to thicken sauce
> Start prepping for your pizza creation
> Now go to the TOC for your selection of Pizza Toppings **(pg. 69)**

LOWER IN FAT ALFREDO SAUCE

This sauce is similar to béchamel, but it is way creamier and cheesier. For those who love cheese, this is the great sauce for them.

Total Time: 15 minutes
Makes: 2 cups

INGREDIENTS:
¼ cup butter
¼ cup all-purpose flour
½ tsp. garlic salt
2 cup half and half
2 garlic cloves, minced
1 tbsp. parsley flakes, dried
1/3 cup Parmesan cheese, grated

DIRECTIONS:
❯ Pour the butter in a saucepan
❯ Melt the butter over medium heat
❯ Stir in the flour and garlic salt and mix smoothly
❯ Gradually beat the half and half in the sauce
❯ Stir in the garlic, parsley and Parmesan cheese
❯ Continue to stir
❯ Bring the sauce to a simmer and cook for 5 minutes
❯ Make sure the sauce has thickened
❯ Start prepping for your pizza creation
❯ Now go to the TOC for your selection of Pizza Toppings **(pg. 69)**

FIERY SPANISH ROMESCO SAUCE

This is one of those sauces that pairs with almost anything. Don't feel like you can't be creative here. Toss some chicken, shrimp, steak and vegetables on your pie and you will wonder why you didn't switch your sauce earlier.

Total Time: 5 minutes

Makes: 1 cup

INGREDIENTS:

1 7-oz. jar roasted red peppers, drained
1 slice sandwich bread, lightly toasted
¼ cup silvered almonds, toasted
1 tsp. Sherry vinegar
1 garlic clove
1 tbsp. olive oil
1 small jalapeno pepper, seeded
¼ tsp. ancho chili powder
½ tsp. paprika
½ tsp. kosher salt

DIRECTIONS:

> Equipment needed: Food processor
> Toast the silvered almonds at 350 for 3 minutes
> Pour all of the ingredients into the food processor
> Blend smoothly
> Taste and adjust the seasonings as needed
> Start prepping for your pizza creation
> Now go to the TOC for your selection of Pizza Toppings **(pg. 69)**

SECTION 10: PIZZA TOPPINGS / LET'S GET CREATIVE:

PLEASE NOTE: At this stage, your crust is made and you've picked your sauce. Remember not to use too much sauce. Pour over the crust thick and spread evenly. Cook time for your pizzas will be around 12-14 minutes. Depending on the type of oven you have this may vary, so just look for the cheese to melt and the crust to be browned. Enjoy! :)

THE ORIGINAL NEOPOLITAN

This pizza is known as the pizza that left Italy and made it to America. It is the pie that made Americans crazy for pizza and you and your family will not be disappointed.

RECCOMENDED:

RISING PIZZA DOUGH – REFER TO PAGE 29 OF PIZZA CRUST SECTION OR CHOOSE THE CRUST OF YOUR CHOICE

GARLIC AND OLIVE OIL SAUCE – REFER TO PAGE 56 OF PIZZA SAUCE SECTION OR CHOOSE THE CRUST OF YOUR CHOICE

TOPPINGS:

12 oz. buffalo mozzarella
6 tbsp. extra virgin olive oil
24 basil leaves
Salt, to taste

Cooking: 12-14 min. Oven types may vary. Look for melted cheese & browning.

SUNNY CALIFORNIA STYLE

The sun is always shining in California. At least that is what they say. Why should your pizza be any different? This Sunny California Style pizza will definitely brighten up your day.

RECCOMENDED:

CALIFLOWER CRUST – REFER TO PAGE 36 OF PIZZA CRUST SECTION OR CHOOSE THE CRUST OF YOUR CHOICE

SAVORY PUMPKIN PUREE SAUCE – REFER TO PAGE 49 OF PIZZA SAUCE SECTION OR CHOOSE THE CRUST OF YOUR CHOICE

TOPPINGS:

1 ½ cups Monterey Jack Cheese, shredded
2 cups cooked chicken, cut up
½ cup sliced ripe olives
1 medium avocado, sliced
1 fresh lemon, juice

Cooking: 12-14 min. Oven types may vary. Look for melted cheese & browning

CHICAGO – THIN CRUST STYLE

The taste of Chicago Style Pizza on a thin crust! Something you can make at home on your very own pizza stone. You won't have to take any trips to Chicago to taste this masterpiece.

RECCOMENDED:

THIN CRUST – REFER TO PAGE 31 OF PIZZA CRUST SECTION OR CHOOSE THE CRUST OF YOUR CHOICE

PINE NUTTY PESTO SAUCE – REFER TO PAGE 45 OF PIZZA SAUCE SECTION OR CHOOSE THE CRUST OF YOUR CHOICE

TOPPINGS:

¾ cups mozzarella cheese, shredded
¾ cups cheddar, shredded
1 cup fennel- laced Italian Sausage
1 cup Italian beef
1 cup pepperoni
½ cup pepperchini's
Parmesan, shredded to taste
Romano, shredded to taste

Cooking: 12-14 min. Oven types may vary. Look for melted cheese & browning

By: A.J. Luigi

GREEK STYLE PIZZA

Greece is full of many incredible ingredients. The freshness and brightness of the ingredients makes you feel like you are relaxing by the Mediterranean Sea.

RECCOMENDED:

WHOLE WEAT DOUGH – REFER TO PAGE 39 OF PIZZA CRUST SECTION OR CHOOSE THE CRUST OF YOUR CHOICE

HUM FOR HUMMUS STYLE PIZZA SAUCE – REFER TO PAGE 50 OF PIZZA SAUCE SECTION OR CHOOSE THE CRUST OF YOUR CHOICE

TOPPINGS:

1 cup cooked lamb, cut into strips
1 red onion, sliced
4 oz. fresh spinach, roughly chopped
2 red pepper halves, roughly chopped
¾ cup Kalamata olives, halved
6 oz. feta cheese, crumbled

Cooking: 12-14 min. Oven types may vary. Look for melted cheese & browning

ST. LOUIS STYLE

This pizza is so close to New York Style pizza, except for the crust. This super thin yeast-less crust is cut in squares and piled high with some of your favorite cheeses and toppings.

RECCOMENDED:

ST. LOUIS STYLE PIZZA CRUST - REFER TO PAGE 34 OF PIZZA CRUST SECTION OR CHOOSE THE CRUST OF YOUR CHOICE

NO TOMATO IN THIS TOMATO SAUCE - REFER TO PAGE 51 OF PIZZA SAUCE SECTION OR CHOOSE THE CRUST OF YOUR CHOICE

TOPPINGS:

1 cup white cheddar cheese, shredded
½ cup Swiss cheese, shredded
½ cup provolone cheese, shredded
1 tsp. liquid hickory liquid smoke
2 tsp. oregano
2 tsp. basil
1 tsp. thyme
½ red onion
½ green pepper
½ cup sausage
½ cup cooked hamburger meat
½ cup pepperoni
½ cup bacon
¾ cup mushrooms
½ cup black olives
¼ cup anchovy
½ cup Canadian bacon
¼ cup jalapenos
½ cup pineapples

½ cup banana peppers
½ cup tomatoes

Cooking: 12-14 min. Oven types may vary. Look for melted cheese & browning

THAI CHICKEN STYLE PIZZA

The sweet and spicy flavors of Thai cuisine pair well with any type of dough: whether in a sandwich or on pizza dough. The crunchiness of the peanuts with the bean sprouts will give you a different definition of pizza.

RECCOMENDED:

BEET STYLE PIZZA CRUST - REFER TO PAGE 41 OF PIZZA CRUST SECTION OR CHOOSE THE CRUST OF YOUR CHOICE

THAI PEANUT SAUCE - REFER TO PAGE 62 OF PIZZA SAUCE SECTION OR CHOOSE THE CRUST OF YOUR CHOICE

TOPPINGS:

1 tbsp. olive oil
2 chicken breasts cut into cubes
2 cups mozzarella cheese, shredded
4 green onions, slivered diagonally
½ cup bean sprouts
1/3 cup shredded carrot
2 tbsp. roasted peanuts, chopped
2 tbsp. fresh cilantro, chopped

Cooking: 12-14 min. Oven types may vary. Look for melted cheese & browning

MEXICAN STYLE PIZZA

The zesty taste of salsa smothered on dough, and topped with beans, avocado and sour cream gives you the illusion of eating a chewy, savory taco.

RECCOMENDED:

CRACKER PIZZA CRUST – REFER TO PAGE 33 OF PIZZA CRUST SECTION OR CHOOSE THE CRUST OF YOUR CHOICE

ZESTY SALSA RECIPE – REFER TO PAGE 47 OF PIZZA SAUCE SECTION OR CHOOSE THE CRUST OF YOUR CHOICE

TOPPINGS:

1 16 oz. can refried beans
1 lb. ground beef
1 package taco seasoning mix
2 cups cheddar cheese, shredded
8 tbsp. sour cream
2 Roma tomatoes, chopped
2 green onions, chopped
1 4 oz. can diced green chilies, drained
½ avocado, diced
1 tbsp. black olives, sliced

Cooking: 12-14 min. Oven types may vary. Look for melted cheese & browning

NEW ORLEANS MUFFALETTA STYLE PIZZA

This pizza combines all the flavors of the famous sandwich on top of dough. The toppings include lots of meat, olives, cheese, peppers and garlic. This is one hearty and delicious pizza.

RECCOMENDED:

ZUCCHINI CRUST – REFER TO PAGE 37 OF PIZZA CRUST SECTION OR CHOOSE THE CRUST OF YOUR CHOICE

BLACK OLIVE TAPENADE SAUCE – REFER TO PAGE 53 OF PIZZA SAUCE SECTION OR CHOOSE THE CRUST OF YOUR CHOICE

TOPPINGS:

Olive salad
½ cup mixed chopped olives
¼ cup chopped roasted red peppers
¼ cup chopped marinated artichoke hearts
2 tbsp. olive oil
1 tbsp. red wine vinegar
2 garlic cloves, minced
¼ tsp. red pepper flakes
¼ tsp. dried oregano

Other toppings
½ cup shredded mozzarella
3 slices provolone cheese, cut into strips
3 slices salami, cut into strips
3 slices Mortadella, cut into strips
3 slices Capicolla Prosciutto, cut into strips

Cooking: 12-14 min. Oven types may vary. Look for melted cheese & browning

HAWAIIAN STYLE PIZZA

Everyone loves Hawaiian Barbeque. How about tossing some of that Kalua pork and green onions on your pie? You will fill like you are watching the Hawaiian sunset when you bite into this masterpiece.

RECCOMENDED:

RISING PIZZA DOUGH – REFER TO PAGE 29 OF PIZZA CRUST SECTION OR CHOOSE THE CRUST OF YOUR CHOICE

SWEET AND TANGY BARBEQUE SAUCE – REFER TO PAGE 48 OF PIZZA SAUCE SECTION OR CHOOSE THE CRUST OF YOUR CHOICE

TOPPINGS:

2 cups Kalua Pork
3 oz. Fontina, grated
1 oz. Parmesan, grated
1 ½ cup mozzarella cheese, shredded
6 strips bacon, diced
1 20 oz. can pineapple chunks, drained
½ cup bell pepper, thinly sliced
¼ cup green onion, sliced
¼ cup red onion, diced
2 tbsp. cilantro, chopped

Cooking: 12-14 min. Oven types may vary. Look for melted cheese & browning

PISSALADIERE FRENCH STYLE PIZZA

This pizza will pair well with a thin crust and the caramelized onion sauce. The ingredients on this pie will melt in your mouth and having you explore different types of pizza.

RECCOMENDED:

THIN CRUST – REFER TO PAGE 31 OF PIZZA CRUST SECTION OR CHOOSE THE CRUST OF YOUR CHOICE

CARMELIZED ONION SAUCE – REFER TO PAGE 59 OF PIZZA SAUCE SECTION OR CHOOSE THE CRUST OF YOUR CHOICE

TOPPINGS:

1 ½ large onions, sliced
3 anchovy filets, chopped
1 garlic clove, minced
6 Kalamata, green and black olives, halved and pitted
Thyme, for garnish

Cooking: 12-14 min. Oven types may vary. Look for melted cheese & browning

By: A.J. Luigi

SALAD SYTLE PIZZA
The taste of summer in your mouth! This tangy Italian chopped salad will provide a freshness that you never thought would go on top of any pie.

RECOMMENDED:
FLATBREAD PIZZA CRUST – REFER TO PAGE 40 OF PIZZA CRUST SECTION OR CHOOSE THE CRUST OF YOUR CHOICE

GARLIC AIOLI PIZZA SAUCE – REFER TO PAGE 56 OF PIZZA SAUCE SECTION OR CHOOSE THE CRUST OF YOUR CHOICE

TOPPINGS:
2 cups mozzarella cheese
1 cup romaine lettuce, shredded
½ cup chickpeas
6 cherry tomatoes, sliced
3 slices of salami, stripped
4 pepperoncini, diced
¼ olives, chopped
Parsley, to taste
Basil, to taste
Feta cheese, to taste
Parmesan, to taste

Cooking: 12-14 min. Oven types may vary. Look for melted cheese & browning

MIAMI-CUBAN STYLE PIZZA

The taste of Miami on a pie! The crunchiness of the corn, mixed with the beans, and cheese leaves for a nice, healthy and hearty meal.

RECOMMENDED:

EGGPLANT PIZZA CRUST – REFER TO PAGE 42 OF PIZZA CRUST SECTION OR CHOOSE THE CRUST OF YOUR CHOICE

MIDDLE EASTERN ZAATAR SAUCE – REFER TO PAGE 61 OF PIZZA SAUCE SECTION OR CHOOSE THE CRUST OF YOUR CHOICE

TOPPINGS:

1 110-oz can whole-kernel corn, drained
½ tsp. cumin seeds
1 cups roasted chicken breast, diced
1 15-oz. can black beans, rinsed and drained
1 garlic clove, minced
2 tbsp. fresh lemon juice
¾ cup Monterey Jack cheese with jalapeno peppers
4 tsp. fresh cilantro, chopped

Cooking: 12-14 min. Oven types may vary. Look for melted cheese & browning

GERMAN SAUSAGE PIZZA

German is known for their beer and for their bratwurst. Two ingredients that you would never think would go with pizza. Well in this pie, we mix apricot preserves, with sauerkraut and bratwurst. Let us know what you think.

RECOMMENDED:

SWEET POTATO PIZZA CRUST – REFER TO PAGE 43 OF PIZZA CRUST SECTION OR CHOOSE THE CRUST OF YOUR CHOICE

BASIL AND SUN-DRIED TOMATO SAUCE – REFER TO PAGE 65 OF PIZZA SAUCE SECTION OR CHOOSE THE CRUST OF YOUR CHOICE

TOPPINGS:

1/3 cup apricot preserves
8 oz. uncooked bratwurst links, casings removed
1 large onion, chopped
1 cup sauerkraut, drained
1 ½ cup Monterey Jack cheese, shredded

Cooking: 12-14 min. Oven types may vary. Look for melted cheese & browning

WHITE CLAM STYLE PIZZA

If you want to try something different then try this pizza. With a thin crust, and a creamy Alfredo sauce. This pie will be one of the most appealing things you have ever tasted.

RECOMMENDED:

RISING DOUGH PIZZA CRUST – REFER TO PAGE 29 OF PIZZA CRUST SECTION OR CHOOSE THE CRUST OF YOUR CHOICE

CREAMY BECHAMEL SAUCE – REFER TO PAGE 46 OF PIZZA SAUCE SECTION OR CHOOSE THE CRUST OF YOUR CHOICE

TOPPINGS:

24 littleneck clams, scrubbed, shucked
1 wedge Pecorino-Romano cheese
1 handful of fresh oregano
4 garlic cloves, sliced
Extra virgin olive oil, to taste

Cooking: 12-14 min. Oven types may vary. Look for melted cheese & browning

BREAKFAST STYLE PIZZA

This pizza is something you can eat any time of the day. Scrambled eggs, sausage and hash browns go great on high rising dough.

RECOMMENDED:

FLATBREAD PIZZA CRUST – REFER TO PAGE 40 OF PIZZA CRUST SECTION OR CHOOSE THE CRUST OF YOUR CHOICE

FIERY SPANISH ROMESCO SAUCE – REFER TO PAGE 68 OF PIZZA SAUCE SECTION OR CHOOSE THE CRUST OF YOUR CHOICE

TOPPINGS:

6 eggs, scrambled
1 lb. ground breakfast sausage
1 cup frozen hash browns, thawed
1 package bacon bits
1 cup Monterey Jack cheese, shredded
1 cup cheddar cheese, shredded

Cooking: 12-14 min. Oven types may vary. Look for melted cheese & browning

CHICKEN ALFREDO STYLE PIZZA

A classic Italian favorite dish can now be found on top of a pizza crust. The gooiness of the cheese, the creaminess of the Alfredo sauce, mixed with the spinach and tomatoes will pop in your mouth.

RECOMMENDED:

THIN CRUST – REFER TO PAGE 31 OF PIZZA CRUST SECTION OR CHOOSE THE CRUST OF YOUR CHOICE

LOWER IN FAT ALFREDO SAUCE – REFER TO PAGE 67 OF PIZZA SAUCE SECTION OR CHOOSE THE CRUST OF YOUR CHOICE

TOPPINGS:

1 garlic clove, minced
1 tsp. red pepper flakes
¼ cup Parmesan, grated
2 cups baby spinach, well washed and dried
1 cup grape tomatoes, red and yellow
1 cup mozzarella, grated
1 boneless skinless chicken breast, cubed
Salt, to taste
Pepper, to taste

Cooking: 12-14 min. Oven types may vary. Look for melted cheese & browning

MEAT LOVERS STYLE PIZZA

Can't decide on what type of meat to put on your pie! Don't worry about it. This is your chance to top your pizza with all of the meat that you want.

RECOMMENDED:

HIGH RISING DOUGH – REFER TO PAGE 29 OF PIZZA CRUST SECTION OR CHOOSE THE CRUST OF YOUR CHOICE

GO BACK TO THE BASICS TOMATO SAUCE – REFER TO PAGE 60 OF PIZZA SAUCE SECTION OR CHOOSE THE CRUST OF YOUR CHOICE

TOPPINGS:

1/2 lb. lean ground beef
½ lb. bulk Italian sausage
½ cup pepperoni, sliced
1 oz. thinly sliced deli salami, cut into quarters
½ cup Canadian bacon, diced
1 cup cheddar cheese, shredded
1 cup mozzarella cheese, shredded

Cooking: 12-14 min. Oven types may vary. Look for melted cheese & browning

VEGGIE STYLE PIZZA

There are some days when the idea of meat doesn't sound appealing. Or maybe you don't meat at all. Whatever the reason, this pie will satisfy all of your veggie craving needs.

RECOMMENDED:

THIN CRUST – REFER TO PAGE 31 OF PIZZA CRUST SECTION OR CHOOSE THE CRUST OF YOUR CHOICE

PEPPERY JELLY PIZZA SAUCE – REFER TO PAGE 57 OF PIZZA SAUCE SECTION OR CHOOSE THE CRUST OF YOUR CHOICE

TOPPINGS:

½ small onion, chopped
1 15-oz can tomatoes, diced
1 garlic clove, finely chopped
1 ¼ cup mozzarella cheese, shredded
½ cup green bell pepper, chopped
1.2 cup fresh mushrooms, sliced
¼ cup cheddar cheese, shredded

Cooking: 12-14 min. Oven types may vary. Look for melted cheese & browning

EVERYTHING STYLE PIZZA

Sometimes you just don't know what you want. This particular pizza has a little bit of everything. This way you can appease your taste buds.

RECOMMENDED:

CRACKER STYLE CRUST – REFER TO PAGE 33 OF PIZZA CRUST SECTION OR CHOOSE THE CRUST OF YOUR CHOICE

CARROT CHILI PASTE SAUCE – REFER TO PAGE 54 OF PIZZA SAUCE SECTION OR CHOOSE THE CRUST OF YOUR CHOICE

TOPPINGS:

½ cup lean ground beef, cooked and drained
1/3 cup Canadian bacon, thinly sliced
1/3 cup pepperoni, thinly sliced
2 cups fresh mushrooms, sliced
2 cups sweet green bell pepper, thinly sliced
2 cups red onion, thinly sliced
2 cups fresh baby spinach
2 tbsp. Kalamata olives, sliced and pitted
1 cup mozzarella cheese, shredded
1 cup cheddar cheese, shredded

Cooking: 12-14 min. Oven types may vary. Look for melted cheese & browning

GRILLED EVERYTHING STYLE PIZZA

This is one of those sauces that pairs with almost anything. Don't feel like you can't be creative here. Toss some chicken, shrimp, steak and vegetables on your pie and you will wonder why you didn't switch your sauce earlier.

RECOMMENDED:

THIN CRUST PIZZA CRUST - REFER TO PAGE 31 OF PIZZA CRUST SECTION OR CHOOSE THE CRUST OF YOUR CHOICE

GARLIC AIOLI SAUCE - REFER TO PAGE 64 OF PIZZA SAUCE SECTION OR CHOOSE THE CRUST OF YOUR CHOICE

TOPPINGS:

8 oz. fresh mozzarella, sliced
½ cup roasted peppers, sliced
4 oz. Capicola thinly sliced and torn
1 cup micro greens
1 cup pea shoots
1 cup baby greens
½ bunch fresh basil, torn

Cooking: 12-14 min. Oven types may vary. Look for melted cheese & browning

By: A.J. Luigi

CHARTS FOR HOME COOKING

FOOD TEMPERATURES FOR SAFE HEATING, DANGER CHILLING & FREEZING ZONES!

A guide for food temperature cooking!

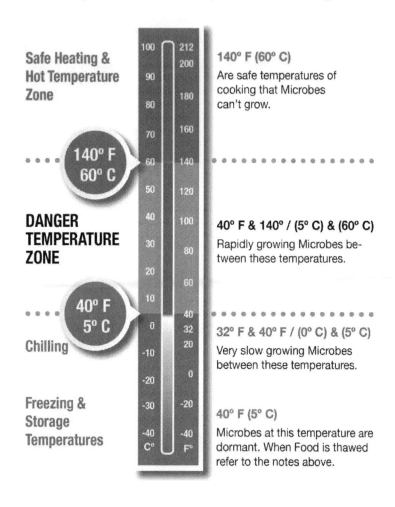

Safe Heating & Hot Temperature Zone

140° F (60° C)
Are safe temperatures of cooking that Microbes can't grow.

DANGER TEMPERATURE ZONE

40° F & 140° / (5° C) & (60° C)
Rapidly growing Microbes between these temperatures.

Chilling

32° F & 40° F / (0° C) & (5° C)
Very slow growing Microbes between these temperatures.

Freezing & Storage Temperatures

40° F (5° C)
Microbes at this temperature are dormant. When Food is thawed refer to the notes above.

MEAT BAKING CHART TEMPERATURES!

BAKING	TEMPERATURE	COOKING TIME
BEEF		
Sirloin or Rib Roast	325 degrees	20-25 minutes
Rump, Round (Roast)	275 degrees	45-50 minutes
VEAL		
Leg, Loin, Rib Roast	325 degrees	35-40 minutes
PORK		
Leg or Loin	325 degrees	20-25 minutes
Crown Roast	325 degrees	15-20 minutes
Shoulder Roast	325 degrees	25-30 minutes
HAM		
Smoked, Pre-Cooked	325 degrees	10-15 minutes
LAMB		
Leg	350-400 degrees	20-25 minutes
Leg, Shoulder Roast	325 degrees	25-30 minutes
Rack (Roast)	400 degrees	20-25 minutes
POULTRY		
Turkey	325 degrees	4-5 hrs / 10-14lbs
Chicken	375 degrees	2.5-3.5hrs / 4-6lbs
Duckling	325-350 degrees	2-3 hrs / 4-5 lbs
Capon	325-350 degrees	2.5-3.5hrs /6-8lbs
Goose	325 degrees	4-5 hrs / 10-12lbs

FRYING CHART

Reason for the frying chart. – We understand that everything you cook won't be a pizza so we added this temperature chart for you to use with your other cooking needs.

FRYING	TEMPERATURE	COOKING TIME
Bacon	300-325 degrees	8-10 minutes
Canadian bacon	275-300 degrees	3-4 minutes
Chicken	325-350 degrees	25-40 minutes
Eggs, fried	250-275 degrees	3-5 minutes
Eggs, scrambled	250-275 degrees	3-5 minutes
Fish	325-375 degrees	5-10 minutes
French Toast	300-325 degrees	4-6 minutes
Ham ½ thick	325-350 degrees	10-12 minutes
Ham ¾ thick	325-350 degrees	14-16 minutes
Hamburgers	325-375 degrees	8-12 minutes
Minute Steak	375-400 degrees	4-5 minutes
Pork Chops ½ thick	325-375 degrees	15-20 minutes
Pork Chops ¾ thick	325-375 degrees	20-25 minutes
Potatoes	300-350 degrees	10-12 minutes
Sausage, link	300-325 degrees	20-30 minutes
Sausage, precooked	325-350 degrees	10-12 minutes
Sandwiches, grilled	300-325 degrees	5-10 minutes
Steak, rare	350-400 degrees	6-7 minutes
Steak, medium	350-400 degrees	10-12 minutes

NEXT ON THE LIST!

HERE'S WHAT YOU DO NOW...

If you were pleased with our book then please leave us a review on amazon where you purchased this book! In the world of an author who writes books independently, your reviews are not only touching but important so that we know you like the material we have prepared for "you" our audience! So, leave us a review...we would love to see that you enjoyed our book!

If for any reason that you were less than happy with your experience then send me an email at **Info@RecipeNerds.com** and let me know how we can better your experience. We always come out with a few volumes of our books and will possibly be able to address some of your concerns. Do keep in mind that we strive to do our best to give you the highest quality of what "we the independent authors" pour our heart and tears into.

I am very happy to create new and exciting recipes and do appreciate your purchase. I thank you for your many great reviews and comments! With a warm heart! ~A.J. Luigi "Professional Loving Chef"

ABOUT THE AUTHOR

A.J. Luigi is a Professional Gourmet Italian Chef that has over 25 years of experience in his craft as a Chef. He moved to the States as a young boy and created a passion for cooking for his large family! From this experience, he has created this special recipe book just for you! These special recipes within this book are some of his very own personal favorites that he has shared with you, his audience. His profession calls for her to visit many well-known names to cater special events and whip up some of the best dishes he can offer. In his spare time, he enjoys travel, walks on the beach and perfecting his craft, creating new and delicious recipes, with you in mind! Enjoy!

QUICK START GUIDE

GET YOUR QUICK START
GRILLING GUIDE

EASY AS 1 - 2 - 3

A SIMPLE STEP GUIDE FOR MAKING
PIZZA STONE PIZZA ON THE GRILL!

Learn the basics when grilling your stone! This quick start guide will show you the proper way to get your pizza stone on the grill and baking your pizzas in no time! **Get yours NOW** by just simply clicking the button below! Hope you enjoy!

http://eepurl.com/dsZ_NP

STONE PIZZA CREATION RECIPES & NOTES:

Create your very own "Marvelous Masterpieces". Log them in this section. You will be amazed on how many ideas you come up with! **Now get creating!**

Pizza Name	Crust	Sauce	Toppings

STONE PIZZA CREATION RECIPES & NOTES:

Create your very own "Marvelous Masterpieces". Log them in this section. You will be amazed on how many ideas you come up with! **Now get creating!**

Pizza Name	Crust	Sauce	Toppings

Made in the USA
Middletown, DE
19 December 2022

19494394R00061